I0036584

Contents

Tractors replace not only mules but people. They cultivate to the very door of the houses of those whom they replace.

Dorothea Lange and Paul S Taylor

An American Exodus. A record of human erosion, 1939

Photo: **Tractored out. Dorothea Lange, 1938**

Foreword

Too often commentaries about how to reform the NHS are provided by those who have a vested interest in trying to change it. Rarely do we listen to those who have a long experience of working in the NHS and who simply want to share what they've learned. This has led to decades of pointless structural reform, often disguising the growing power of Whitehall and those who seek commercial gain.

One of the consequences of the endless search for a new system, the panacea of structural reform, is that those who actually work in the system become increasingly cynical, mistrustful and depressed. Some change may be inevitable, but change for the sake of political posturing and privatisation does not create the best basis for innovation, trust and hopefulness.

In this paper David Zigmond illuminates the internal factors that ensure the effectiveness of the NHS: relationships of trust, closeness to community, and a human scale. All of these have been sacrificed by those who have imposed phoney competition, privatisation and bureaucratic regulations on the NHS. However, even important allies of the NHS, like the King's Fund, struggle to understand what really matters to the people who use and work in the NHS. Too often we turn people into robots - mere agents of our good intentions. We forget that bigger is not always better.

It is time to stop trying to reform the NHS and instead to listen to those who use it and those who work in it. In particular it is time to reclaim our humanity and end the commercialised industrialisation of healthcare.

Simon Duffy

Director of the Centre for Welfare Reform

Introduction

Just as modern mass production requires the standardisation of commodities, so the social process requires standardisation of man, and this standardisation is called equality.

Erich Fromm (1956) The Art of Loving

In 2014 the King's Fund published a widely discussed and respected report *Reforming the NHS from Within: Beyond hierarchy, inspection and markets*. Many of its observations and conclusions have become even more relevant and accurate, and so merit our review and careful attention.

The King's Fund's analysis is of available data of systems' performance. The report shows how the increase of top-down micromanagement, regulations and inspections has mostly increased costs without yielding better performance. Conclusions about the effects of foisted and complex marketisation of services is similar.

What can we usefully add to this? This is an important question because the King's Fund is a powerfully influential body, so its oversights are likely to be adopted and perpetuated by any reformer of our cumulatively specious reforms. So what is missing from the King's Fund's report?

Reforming the NHS from Within does characteristically sterling work with systems analysis but its view is limited by its method. This is because a statistically-based view is necessarily confined to that of organisational performance, not personal and social experience – something more elusive to statistics and data.

This paper here first summarises the King's Fund's formulations and then expands these, to consider the personal and social consequences of our problematic healthcare reforms. Such experiential speculations must draw from personal narratives and reports quite as much as statistics and data: we here need a mixture of qualitative as well as quantitative research.

This paper thus uses authentic vignettes and reports to illustrate, or speculate about, the more humanly sentient aspects of our problems of care. In seeking these larger views of our troubled systems, we must listen carefully to the voices of those individuals who inhabit them. For instance:

"I was asked recently what I thought were the main changes I had witnessed in the NHS since the end of the 1960s, 'Everything to do with machines and technology has got better, most things to do with human relationships and understanding is worse', I answered quickly. This was a brief conversation, so there was much more I did not say: for example, that variation is less, so management, reliability and safety are often greater… but that these efficiencies are paid for by an overall loss of much that was valued, for many decades, by both NHS staff and patients."

This is a typical utterance of a veteran frontline, NHS doctor. Almost all talk with disillusioned fatigue of the recent decades' serial reforms: how although, sometimes, in its machine-like operations the NHS may claim to function better; in its human experiences and matrices it does not.

1. Treating the NHS like a machine

What is the evidence that the NHS-as-a-machine has become more widely efficient over the decades? Proof, or even clear inference, is often patchy and inconsistent. What *Reforming the NHS from Within* does assert with solid clarity is that successive reforms dating from the Thatcher-era have rarely yielded the promised benefits or economies.

What is the nature of these contended reforms? The King's Fund identifies three main driving and guiding forces:

1. Targets and performance management
2. Inspection and regulation
3. Competition and choice

Much of that report then carefully analyses and explains how this three pronged solution is externally imposed and managed: and then how it has added very substantially to complexity and thus to the cost of the services. All this happens, the King's Fund concludes, with usually no evident longer-term benefit – and sometimes with perverse consequences.

It is the perverse consequences, in particular, that this paper explores here. For it is these that account for much of our healthcare's increasing personal and social malaise and staffing instability.

To further describe and designate the perverse consequences of these reforms I have developed a slightly different account of the problem and one which I have analysed in detail in my various publications on my own website.

There are 3 sets of faulty assumptions which underpin the various 'reform' efforts:

1. **The 4Cs** = Competition, Commerced Commissioning and Commodification.
2. **REMIC** = Remote Management, Inspection and Compliance. Good analogies here are the largely robotic factory or air traffic control centre.
3. **Gigantism** = The mandate, whenever possible, to merged and ever-larger units (eg hospitals and GP surgeries).

Gigantism is the one principle that receives relatively little attention in the King's Fund report, even though, as we shall see, Gigantism is particularly damaging to personal aspects of healthcare.

Reforming the NHS from Within does, however, express a kindred view: that highly managed and externally imposed changes are often not as effective as more nuanced, maybe slower, changes – those that are encouraged to evolve from within healthcare professions and their organisations.

But should this assertion not be taken further? There is so much evidence that our current *excess* of such external management is not just ineffective: it is increasingly damaging and destructive to the internal motivations, capacities and spirit of healthcarers – the very elements that make otherwise healthy evolution possible.

Academic and research think tanks such as the King's Fund spend much time and resources collecting and patterning data about how public funds are used in our healthcare, and whether these are the best options. So their reports tend to 'big picture' evaluations of efficiency and expenditure.

However, if we wish to understand these problems in a human or experiential way we then need different vantage points. Here longer-term practitioners are excellent witnesses to the incremental depletion of their profession's morale: their spirit, creative intellect, healthy pride and secure attachment in their work. There are many measurable indices, too, of these depletions – shown in rates of sickness, breakdown, burnout, premature retirement, litigation, parlous recruitment – all indicate how serious this is. [To salvage some brevity this paper has not listed here the many references providing supporting statistics. Interested readers can readily consult the reputable sources used. They include: NHS Digital, Office for National Statistics, Social Care Information Centre, British Medical Association and the King's Fund itself.]

Shortly after his promotion (July 2018) the new Secretary of State for Health signalled his alarm at the evidence of endemic bullying within the NHS. Recently published books by NHS doctors, too, have documented personal experiences of these much wider institutional-personal problems. In particular I would recommend Adam Kay's *This is Going to Hurt* and *Admissions: A Life in Brain Surgery* by Henry Marsh.

So *Reforming the NHS from Within* shows clearly how our current systems give us poor efficiency and economics, but stops short of larger questions. How do these reforms become both cause and effect of such poor humanity? And then, how and why are we doing this?

2. Two different kinds of healthcare

Reforming the NHS from Within draws attention to the serious problem of relative (to comparable nations) underfunding. This, belatedly, is now widely recognised by many governing authorities. Yet we need, also, to recognise how we often squander our inadequate funds by inapt usage of our models of management and healthcare. This assertion is less familiar, so needs some definitions and explanation of what our instrumental models are and how we are mis-deploying them.

It is worth making a contrast between two kinds of healthcare:

- **Curative Treatments** (CT) comprise the now-dominant model. They are those encounters where procedural technology has a very high rate of complete problem elimination. Generally leading-edge advances may be transiently controversial, but established practice is not. Examples: Polio vaccine, Appendicectomy, Cataract surgery, Hip replacement. CT is evidently and predominantly scientific in its nature and process.

- **Pastoral healthcare** (PHC), in contrast, is what healthcarers can do when there are no rapidly curative treatments: when we cannot decisively 'fix' with procedures and technology, a problem of health or distress. Yet with knowledge, interest and skill we can instead offer much else: for example, guidance and support of a kind that may induce various kinds of healing, comfort or re-view in the sufferer. This approach (PHC) is a complex mixture of art and science and accounts for: almost all of mental health and a very large part of General Practice, also any care of stress-related, very chronic, terminal and ageing conditions – altogether these probably comprise the larger part of healthcare activity, though not technical resources.

The distinguishing and contrasting characteristics of curative treatments and pastoral healthcare are important to understand. These are clarified overleaf in Table 1.

The King's Fund report does explore this to some degree, drawing on the work of John Seddon and drawing a contrast between command-and-control and systems thinking. What my analysis makes clearer is that if there are any benefits to a command-and-control approach in healthcare it is unlikely to extend to Pastoral Healthcare.

	Curative Treatment (CT)	Pastoral Healthcare (PHC)
Aim	'Fixing' a problem	Comfort, adaptation, skilled guidance, encouragement, subjective compensation
Key word	Treatment	Care
Completability of task	Often. 'Cure'	Less often. 'Good enough'
Art or Science	Predominantly science	Usually complex amalgam of art and science
Type of knowledge	Generic = what is generally true for this group	Idiomorphic = what is true for *this* individual *now*
Deduction or personal imagination?	Mostly deduction	Personal imagination indispensable
Personal knowledge and understanding	Relatively unimportant	Usually crucial
Role of objective diagnosis	Central and mandatory	Often peripheral and relatively disregarded
Human and personal meaning	Unimportant	Central
Insistence on procedure?	Often essential for safety and efficiency	May be destructive to engagement and efficacy
Helped by Gigantism?	Mostly yes	Generally no
Standardisation?	Generally yes	Generally no
Subjective or objective?	Mostly objective	Objectively processed inter-subjectivity
Measurable?	Generally easier	Difficult
Role of personal relationship	Peripheral	Central
Doctor-patient interaction	Didactic	Dialogue, dialectic
Relationships of resources to patient	External (eg conduction of drugs, sutures, stents, prostheses, advice, energy beams, etc)	Internal (eg induction of patients' capacities for immunity, growth, repair, trust, courage, hope, transcendence, etc)
Underlying philosophy	Biological determinism, atomism	Existentialism, humanism, holism
Controllability by REMIC	Easier	Very difficult, can be harmful

Figure 1. Curative Treatment and Pastoral Healthcare

3. The limitations of Curative Treatments

Nothing vast enters the lives of mortals without a curse

Sophocles , 496-406 BC

In the last hundred years the accelerated development of biomedical science – and then its predicated and standardised treatments and prevention programmes – has been historically spectacular. For example, the elimination of numerous lethal contagious infections, the eradicative treatments of many cancers and the prosthetic replacement of our failing parts are all – for the first time ever – what we have often come to expect. The lives of thousands of millions have been assured and their likely fates changed. Inevitably our thinking, and then our culture, change too.

One of these changes in our healthcare culture has been the rise, and then pre-eminence, of the biomechanical model and, therefore, an insistence on a particular kind of evidence. After all, our Curative Treatments have been so extensive and successful why can we not apply these methods across all the problems and dilemmas encountered by healthcarers? Many who espouse this view would assert, partly correctly, that medicine advances by replacing the caprices of pastoral healthcare with the certainties of curative treatments.

This is a complex and very partial truth, yet it has been eagerly and entirely adopted by most healthcare reforms in the last three decades. The consequence is that we have replaced our better – but necessarily more ambiguous – PHC with doomed attempts to process and present them as Curative Treatments. These then function largely as little more than scientifically attired nostrums. These are now well camouflaged and rooted in our healthcare, for they have the appearance – but not the effect – of genuine Curative Treatments. The results are inevitably specious – professionally packaged but often hollow in effect. Examples? There are many such simulacrums to be found amidst mental health diagnoses, procedures and care-pathways where algorithms and administrative systems displace fuller personal understanding. We then come to over-invest in systems apparently rich in data, technical discourse, (over) diagnosis and managed procedures – and so, inversely, impoverished of human sense and engagements. Such quasi-curative treatments are then fraught with confusion, blame and disappointment.

And so it is that the inevitable happens: if we over-invest in the treatment model, we then neglect or even deracinate personal and pastoral healthcare.

This accounts for much of our service's restive and demoralised inefficiency – particularly, as already exampled, in mental health. These problems of staff recruitment, burnout, sickness, premature retirement, intra-organisational litigation, etc are very similar in Mental Health, Primary Care and Social Work and reflect the fact that in these areas Pastoral Healthcare should be the dominant mode of interaction.

As we have noted, it largely accounts, too, for a parallel process: our burgeoning overdiagnosis, and thus over-treatment. A simple internet search for 'overdiagnosis' quickly indicates the vast amount of debate and consternation about this, expressed by both academics and practitioners.

4. The more we can fix, the more we cannot

Seek simplicity, but always mistrust it

Alfred North Whitehead, 1861-1947

This heading - The more we can fix, the more we cannot - as an epithet about healthcare, may sound self-contradictory, and so nonsensical, but it is not. It summarises a growing and inescapable predicament in our individual and social lives; and has become so central as to seriously stymy both our healthcare's profile and aspirations.

What does this mean? And why is it happening?

In the last century we have eliminated or contained a galaxy of previously lethal or crippling diseases. We have 'fixed' them and most of us live much longer.

But the price we pay for this success is often high in several ways. Our later deaths mean longer declines, which means an accumulation of inexorable degenerations which doctors will be less and less able to fix. As curative treatments expand, so too does our need – later in life, maybe – for pastoral healthcare. Eventually our skilled humanity is almost all we have to offer one another.

There is another – I think tragically human – aspect to this conundrum, and it is this: *if we are not struggling to survive, we must search for meaning.* This is as true for societies as it is for individuals. It is a cardinal and growing predicament for post-industrial humanity. In medical terms we can see society enacting this over the decades: for example, in the era of the author's parents' youth GPs' work was more dramatically about survival: a toddler dying of diphtheria, an elderly man blinded by cataracts, a teenager lamed by polio, a young mother doomed by rheumatic heart disease …
all – doctors and patients alike – were more powerless amidst harsher fates. Doctors tried to fix, but usually could not.

That picture has changed dramatically. GPs now can do much more with Curative Treatments, either directly or by referral. Yes, there are some contemporary examples similar to the above, but they are much less common. Yet 'nature abhors a vacuum', so what has filled the gap? Partly our longer, degenerative declines mentioned above; but, quite as much, we are now increasingly troubled – symptomatised and sickened – by our search for meaning and our problems of living. So the GP is now most unlikely to see Rickets – the failure to build an aligned physical skeleton; but most GPs' work is now, in very large part, spent dealing largely with the polymorphic varieties of individuals' difficulties in forming viable *mental* skeletons – secure, stable and satisfying senses of self-amongst-others.

Hence a new tide in our healthcare: an inexorable rise in afflictions of BAMI (Behaviour, Appetite, Mood and Impulse), and the stress-related physical syndromes. Few of these are readily fixable, so are poorly served by Curative Treatments. Yet, in our CT-templated service, that is what, increasingly, we presume to apply. Even more paradoxically our Pastoral Healthcare, which is best suited to addressing such problems, has been largely extinguished by our serial reforms. So we have – by creating an 'illness vacuum' – simultaneously created the space for new forms of health problems to occupy, while systematically driving out the very ways that we might personally contain, guide and heal such problems.

The troubled and ineffective medicalisation of much of psychiatry, and latterly clinical psychology, are prime examples of the misapplication and mushrooming of the CT model amidst the death-by-attrition of PHC. A simple index of this? Consider how few psychiatric patients now know the name of the psychiatrist they last saw. A regime that has yielded us this has clearly sacrificed personal continuity of care to a managed relay of impersonal procedures. Few veteran practitioners would sanction such displacements: in their time they have learned better. What does this portend?

Such misappropriation of therapeutic space is bound to be inefficient, and so it is. And again, we can see how bad humanity is bad economics.

5. What is the role of REMIC?

Not all that counts can be counted; and all that can be counted counts

Albert Einstein

Generally speaking, the 'geography' of the areas of effectiveness (or not) of healthcare micromanagement is indicated by the distinctions of CT and PHC: Curative Treatments are often compatibly and efficiently managed in this way; the opposite is true of Pastoral Healthcare. Here are two contrasting examples:

Curative Treatment - Coronary artery surgery

A coronary artery surgical operating theatre needs clear, precise and rarely variable rules, protocols, regulations and systems of checks and inspections to ensure safety and efficacy. Generally, experts can effectively cascade authoritative instructions to the many differently-tasked workers as to exactly what should be done and when. Variations of personal meaning, motivation or experience in such Curative Treatment procedures are almost entirely irrelevant. Continuity of procedure here is vital; continuity of persons peripheral. If the tight management is courteous, accurate and viable it will arouse little contention.

Pastoral Health Care - Mildred

This example, along with all the others in this paper are from frontline NHS practice: they are real, though disguised.

Mildred is in her early 80s, very active and without serious illness. She has known Dr R, her GP, for fifteen years. Last year her loving husband Ralph died suddenly, from a stroke. Since then Mildred has suffered numerous apparently unrelated minor complaints which Dr R dutifully treats while gently alluding to her grief: Mildred nods in agreement as she swallows and glances at the door with moistening eyes – she politely parries further discussion, and then Dr R's suggestion of counselling.

Dr R has long been struck by Mildred's stoic and introvertedly melancholic demeanour. Years ago she told Dr R that, when she was a teenager, her mother had died in a mental hospital. Yet Mildred, as so often subsequently, had not wanted her painful memory touched directly. So it was when her only child, Stephen, was killed ten years ago, age 40, in an industrial accident. And, Dr R supposes, this is how it is now, in her grief for Ralph.

Mildred takes Dr R's tablets, but not his suggestions for other support or ventilation. Dr R's resonant sadness is tinged with frustration at his self-perceived impotence. 'I only wish there was more I could do for you, Mildred', he says.

'Oh no, doctor. You do me far more good than you can imagine... When shall I see you again?', replies Mildred, dabbing her eyes, as she gathers her coat and bag to depart.

Mildred, it seems, wants her plight understood, yet not talked about explicitly. Dr R now understands this better than ever before. And then Dr R thinks: aren't we all like this, sometimes, in our intimate relationships? Often our most important understandings are not made explicit.

Now Mildred represents a very common type of human problem in General Practice and psychiatry: a person whose persistent distress is not substantially helped by quasi-medical diagnoses and treatments. If we are to understand Mildred we must instead enter a personal hinterland of encoded signals and meanings that lie behind and beyond any standardised procedures, questions and 'evidence'. This – a more bespoke approach – puts meaning and experience at the centre of interactions: none of these can be standardised, mass-produced or micromanaged. We cannot even measure such meaning or experience directly, but are we foolish enough to then deny their existence? Not quite, but almost

In healthcare – and throughout welfare – our reforms have come with increasing rhetorical demands for measurable evidence, objective data and outcomes; for schemata that can be standardised and mass-produced; and for documentation to be always computer-code and data-compatible.

The price we pay for these conventions and protocols? We sacrifice human context and subtext – first the thinking, then the language, and finally the skills or the will to navigate these. The overreach, and then hegemony, of CT emulations into these vast areas has led to the creation of a healthcare culture that is now, so often, perplexingly and painfully unbalanced – technology-rich but humanity-poor; documentation-dense yet dialogue-depleted.

And what can we expect for the Mildreds of the future? It is now most unlikely that, say, in ten years' time a GP, or any healthcarer, would imagine or understand the encoded context or subtext as Dr R was able to do with Mildred. Without such personal continuity of care how could they link her polysymptoms to the unspeakable deaths of Ralph, Stephen and her incarcerated mother? How could the GP then offer that tacitly understood ritualistic healing contact that delicately offered Mildred 'far more good than you can imagine'?

So what will Mildred get instead? A psychotropic drug? More investigations? Referral elsewhere (unattended)? These standardised and managed regimes will be more procedural and more expensive. How will they satisfy either patient or doctor?

6. What about Gigantism?

Gigantism is an important part of our problems; yet receives little attention in Reforming the NHS from Within.

Gigantism, the expedient scaling-up or merging of organisations – in the interests of economy-savings, logistical and management simplification, and pooling of expertise – is often vital to successful manufacturing and retail businesses. Although the limitations of this approach are also now becoming more widely appreciated.

At the beginning of the twentieth century almost all industry adopted Gigantism, command-and-control, top-down management and division of labour as an essential modus operandi, often now referred to as Fordism or Taylorism. At the end of the century the humanly limiting and destructive effects of these were reviewed and reformed, first by Toyota, in Japanese manufacturing industries. These liberations were termed Kaizen and their success is now clear. In contrast, in the UK our Welfare management has moved very much in the opposite direction: we have abandoned the erstwhile trust in autonomous intelligence of a Kaizen-type service, and replaced it with the often-draconian micromanagement and mistrust of Fordism and Taylorism. Our serial Welfare reforms have thus often reversed the kind of progress made in more enlightened sectors of manufacturing industry.

In healthcare the benefits of Gigantism are very uneven: although Curative Treatments are frequently helped by devices of Gigantism, Pastoral Healthcare rarely is. Indeed, in almost all PHC activities Gigantism is likely to be inimical.

So, we can say that with high technology CT interventions Gigantism is almost always – overall – beneficial: intensive care, coronary care, stroke units, neurosurgery are almost all better when aggregated into few but larger operations. Here the pooling of sophisticated expertise and equipment far exceeds considerations of relationships or easy access for visitors, etc.

For example, if a man, Mr AC, develops an acute coronary syndrome and needs an urgent catheter-lab assessment with view to possible insertion of arterial stents, the benefits of the large, pooled-resource specialist centre are indisputable. This highly technical work cannot be efficiently undertaken on an occasional basis in a small, local general hospital.

But this kind of modus operandi has important limits: it is a common misconception to then deduce that such Gigantism should determine all our hospital provision; that we should then close down all small local hospitals or GP practices in the interests of safety and economy.

Consider the following example:

Alfonso and Beatrice are both in their eighties, increasingly frail and struggling with proud pathos to remain both independent and together. Alfonso's diagnoses include moderate heart failure and emphysema, diabetes, macular degeneration and osteoarthritis of his lower limbs and spine. But their greater problem comes from a later development: his Parkinson's disease with dementia.

Alfonso now frequently gets ill beyond Beatrice's capacity to cope, even with good help from the GP and Home Treatment Teams: he freezes, he falls, he gets states of agitated deliria from increasingly frequent chest or urinary infections. The home-systems are not enough; hospital care is needed.

Each time Alfonso is admitted to hospital it is to an enormous airport-like conurbation. Here, each time, he is taken to a different ward under a different team where no one recognises him. Not only that, but the hospital is so large, and the staffing rotas so complex, that the clinical staff rarely know one another well.

In this enormous kaleidoscopic complex Alfonso is processed according to litigation-proof protocol. All plausible investigations are done 'just to be sure'. This includes a brain scan (why?!): Alfonso does not understand this entrapment and flails with agitation. A liaison psychiatrist is added urgently to the growing cauldron of polyspecialists.

Further protocol adds to this cauldron; according to his systematised problems he is referred to the following specialist teams: Geriatrics, Diabetology, Urology, Respiratory Medicine, Falls Clinic, Cardiology, Neurology/Motor Disorders, Dementia/Psychogeriatrics, Liaison Psychiatry and Rehabilitation. Each of these specialists makes a fresh, templated assessment as per NHS Trust protocol. The records achieve impressive but almost unreadable bulk, while the actual, face to face, intercollegial dialogue becomes almost non-existent. No one takes overall responsibility or provides personal continuity of care.5 Meanwhile, the electronic records burgeon to such vast virtual bulk that they become less and less humanly navigable or assimilable ... only a highly-paid lawyer might persist in reading them thoroughly.

Beatrice, meanwhile, is too frail to visit Alfonso easily as the hospital is fifteen miles away. When she does manage the tiring journey, it is to a ward where it is not clear who really knows and understands Alfonso and his (and her) needs. Ten-teamed care is difficult to have a rapport with.

The situation does not improve after Alfonso is ambulanced home. Their erstwhile familiar and friendly small GP surgery has been replaced by a much larger Health Centre where everything seems more remote. Alfonso and Beatrice were informed by an unsigned letter that as 'vulnerable elderly' patients they would have an allocated named doctor. Yet they have never seen this person despite Beatrice's efforts: 'each time we go it's somebody different'.

Fortunately Beatrice's cognition and memory remain excellent. Less fortunately she cannot name a single doctor from Alfonso's ten-teamed hospital stay or her rapidly-carouselled, much-expanded and modernised Health Centre.

In contrast, in 1970 this author worked as a House Physician in a small (by contemporary standards) general hospital, then about a hundred years old. His consultant was Dr A, a general physician who had his own 'firm', ward, nursing and support staff. They cared for many elderly patients who – like Alfonso – had multiple convergent complaints. They provided a complete service – 'general medicine' – which would only call in a tertiary specialist (eg a neurologist, cardiologist, etc) with particularly inscrutable or refractory problems. Dr A and his firm thus dealt with the vaster bulk of problems without such resource. The result? Everyone could know everyone else much better; lines of communication and decision making were shorter and clearer; care was more personally and humanly responsive and intelligent. Contemporary slogans of 'patient-centeredness', 'interprofessional integration' or 'personal continuity of care' did not need galvanising by external experts and initiatives – they grew quietly and naturally from the family-like functioning of Dr A's firm and the personally colleagueial relationships that existed throughout this smaller hospital and beyond ... to the smaller (again) local General Practices who (again) often knew their patients well.

In this context a recent study by Pereira-Gray, published by the BMJ, *Continuity of care with doctors – a matter of life and death? A systematic review of continuity of care and mortality*, is relevant. This is an important and thorough metanalysis published four years after the King's Fund report, shows that continuity of care is crucial, not just for patient satisfaction and reduction of morbidity and hospital admissions, but also overall mortality. This study thus strengthens significantly the arguments here against the 4Cs and Gigantism which are usually inimical to such continuity.

This portrayal of Alfonso, Beatrice and Dr A's erstwhile general medicine merits this long descriptive analysis because such problems now constitute the greater fraction of our acute hospital admissions: such admissions are now mostly for older and frailer persons with convergent degenerative conditions, who need nursing care, recalibration of medication, drips and antibiotics, physiotherapy and reassessment of home services. Most of these do not need complex and expensive scans, an ICU or resuscitation. Many will want visits from similarly aged family or friends nearby. Almost all will respond better to care by people, and in places, that can become familiar enough for personal understanding and trust to develop more easily.

Our better organisational responses to these needs are better found in smaller, more local and personal, hospitals and General Practices, surely? Yet our recent decades' developments have been, almost entirely, in the opposite direction – to fewer and much larger organisations: to conurbated giant hospitals and planned Primary Care Networks. Professionally responsive 'families' become rigidly managed 'factories'; procedures burgeon beyond any human capacity to maintain integrity and human connections get lost; we see more parts but lose sight of the whole.

The costs continue to rise and we sigh wearily amidst our bustling and bewilderment.

7. Can we have too much IT?

It is often assumed that wherever IT can circumvent human activity in a task we should use it: that we will – by ever-expanding computerised systems – reduce human staffing costs, variation, delay and error: we can then concentrate more effectively on our 'core tasks'. A good thing, surely?

Reforming the NHS from Within endorses this widely held view which thus easily segues to policy. That report, as so many of us now do, ignores the many limitations to IT use. This is important because our IT limitations may be subtle yet can be obstructive, even destructive, to our aims – particularly here in Pastoral Healthcare. For example, consider three 'simple' tasks that used to be part of a receptionist's role in traditional and smaller GP surgeries:

- Personally greeting patients, asking simple questions about why have they come. An appointment? For advice? For other information?
- Answering the phone, usually followed by similar questions to the personal greeting (above).
- Taking requests for repeat prescriptions and then liaising with the GP or pharmacist.

On the surface all these tasks can now, seemingly, be unproblematically automated. Screen interactions can greet and process patients and answer their simple queries. The sophisticated answerphone or website similarly greets, guides and books patients. Efficient data systems can check and endorse repeat prescriptions. Who will object to this automation to streamlining and economies? Administrators, managers and doctors have all (mostly) gone with the flow.

'It's progress', we say.

But this expedience then short-circuits some of the more subtle – yet powerful – aspects of our roles, inherent in personal context and subtext. Often, for example, it is very important to people who are lonely, afraid or vulnerable how they are addressed and greeted. The receptionist's voice or manner, for example, may determine whether a person will decide to see a doctor or not, or what kind of a conversation they will then have. As one veteran GP wrote:

'Throughout my long tenure in a small practice I respected and safeguarded my receptionists' roles as social antennae, bridges and buttresses in my contact with patients. Their good sense, warm hearts and kindness helped greatly both my understanding (diagnosis, even) and my therapeutic influence.'

This issue is discussed in more detail in my paper *All is Therapy; All is Diagnosis: Unmapped and perishing latitudes of healthcare*, available on my website.

These beneficent exchanges occurred personally – through the reception hatch, on the phone and when talking about doctors' prescriptions: the overt business was the gateway; the meta-communication – the accompanying personal exchanges – may lead to a related path that is often quite as important.

What is the general principle evinced here? It is that the formulaic demands of zealous IT applications to clinical record keeping and requisite compliance templates, for example, often sacrifice such informal possibilities. While the benefits of IT are readily evident (readability, access, transmission, standardisation) the losses are major but subtle, so often increase insidiously. What does this mean?

Well, we lose sight of those losses: for example the possibility of personal greetings by staff who get to know us. Such subtle loss often means we may eventually perceive the effect, but are not aware of how and when it happened. So computers, in their requirements for codes, data, categories and keywords, will mould or restrict the thinking and language of the operator-practitioner … and also their behaviour. And certainly our IT-dependent era has changed our professional use of language. The kind of qualitative research and literacy imagination amongst doctors, and published by Tavistock Publications in the 1970s, say, has no evident contemporary equivalent.

'The doctor was looking at all this stuff on the computer … no, they didn't seem interested in me, just what was on their screen … even their questions, I think, came from the computer.'

This kind of description of IT-era consultations has become very common, maybe a new norm: it often signals the destruction of the human heart and imagination of pastoral healthcare. Increasingly we are left merely with data and administration.

8. Should we protect doctors from patients?

The more you see of someone, the more of someone you see

There is a commonly expressed notion, iterated in *Reforming the NHS from Within*: doctors are lengthily and expensively trained; we should expect them, therefore, to deal only with important or complex problems. Other 'trivial' or procedural problems can be swiftly despatched elsewhere.

This scheme sounds clear and pragmatic but is based on two unreliable assumptions: (i) that human behaviour is always rational, and (ii) that everything is as it seems. Erstwhile practitioners, who were encouraged to have greater emotional literacy, knew how important it is sometimes to be free of these assumptions.

Here is an example:

Ali seems to want to see Dr F especially, rather than one of the other carouselled doctors sooner. He comes to her with what seem, to her, minor and transient problems: mild hay fever, a small patch of eczema, an occasional fluttering sensation of an eyelid. He appears to her a preoccupied man with a melancholic, somehow pleading, gaze. Why does he want to see her, in particular? She delicately invites him to say more. He declines to be drawn, but then, remarkably, reaches to shake her hand as he leaves.

A year later he comes and tells Dr F a tragic and perilous domestic tale. Sabita, his much-loved wife, no longer loves him. For two years she has progressively distanced herself and he suspects that she has another love. Ali is tangled with intense feelings: lacerated love, powerless rage, lonely fear and reclusive shame. He is now – for the first time ever – drinking heavily and ruminating suicide. All of this is concealed, even from Sabita. No one knows.

'But I can tell you, doctor, I know I can ... you've been very kind to me.'

Two years later Ali is slowly building a new life for himself, without Sabita. He is sad, but thoughtful, appreciative and realistic about the decades and opportunities that lie ahead.

This has not been easy and Dr F has needed other colleagues to help retrieve Ali's resilience, hope and motivation. Yet throughout this Ali has seen Dr F as his primary harbour and anchor-point.

'If I hadn't come to you that time I don't know what would have happened to me … I don't think I'd still be alive', he says to her at his last appointment.

Dr F is wondering, too, what would have happened to Ali had she submitted to the expedience of the carousel?

Such are the kinds of serious problems that may hide and ferment beneath the 'trivial'. Clearly, the subtle human skills that are required to identify and guide such nascent problems are different from those demanded by curative treatments. The importance of this distinction was much better recognised, say, forty years ago. Then, the kind of pastoral healthcare enacted by Dr F with Ali – our better 'family doctoring' – had been recently explored, crystallised and galvanised by the work of Michael Balint. He was a psychoanalyst who made a long-term study, with GPs, of how expanding personal knowledge and understanding with patients greatly enhanced both therapeutic influence and practitioner morale. For two decades these interests and skills burgeoned to raise the morale and recruitment in General Practice, until the 1980s.

The equally rapid rise and decline of influence of the 'Balint Movement' in General Practice can tell us much about our healthcare predicaments. This is explored more fully in my article *From Balint to Square-bashing: Fifty years of General Practice* in the British Journal of General Practice. In addition, Pereira-Gray's type of research could be very helpfully extended to explore whether continuity of personal care may be related to other variables, eg the size of GP surgeries and hospitals and whether the institutions are subject to short-term commissioned contracts etc.

But since then this kind of care has become increasingly unfeasible. Why? Because such care must have roots in ready access to personal continuity from the kind of doctors who have the head-space, the heart-space and the administrative support to provide this. Generally this means vocationally-minded practitioners working in smaller units with good staff stability. Yet the 4Cs, REMIC and Gigantism all pull our culture in another direction. Our reforms have rendered such care almost extinct.

So Pastoral Healthcare perishes; doctors' morale plummets; mental health services buckle as pundits talk of 'prevention' and 'integrated services'.

9. Transformation or evolution?

The word 'transformation' is used several times by the King's Fund report, presumably to connote something bold and undeniably good.

But we should be nervous: we have often heard this word from politicians and senior executives over three decades of successive reconfigurations. Each reform is heralded by a phalanx of similar hypnotic-rhetorical words and slogans vaunting a new and better regime: among these *transformation* is a key word – *this time it will be different* is the meta-message.

Well it was a bit different each time, but rarely in the way wanted and planned. The Health and Social Care Act (2012) is an egregious, currently wounding example. Precedents for radical, even revolutionary, zealous transformations show us a familiar historical pattern that is often depressing, sometimes chilling.

Yet the parliamentary mandate for the formation of the NHS in 1948 was a rare, wise and true transformation: an initiative of blessed boldness that few now dispute. Recent reforms – other kinds of transformations – have clearly had very different yields.

Now-retiring NHS doctors saw previous improvements of a more gentle, stable and sustainable kind. They describe a relatively human world before such hierarchies, inspections and markets (the triad of the King's Fund report's subtitle). Innate capacities and vocations were recognised, gently encouraged, guided … and (mostly) trusted.

A better word for those kind of changes is evolution, not transformation. Evolution may better conserve that imperilled trust.

10. What should we do differently?

What are the kind of things that we can do to reclaim some of our better human sense, understanding and connection? How may we thus assure our better Pastoral Healthcare and – inseparably – the well-motivated good health of our practitioners? For necessary brevity these listed suggestions are merely outlined, not expounded – greater detail is found elsewhere.

Are these changes 'transformational'? They are probably better termed as ecological or conservationist: reclaiming, enabling and protecting the more natural human eco-systems that can grow in sustainable ways, yet – as we have witnessed so painfully over the last thirty years – are so prone to destruction by zealously applied industrial-type processes. So, like much environmentalism, these suggestions are about the retrieval, and then stewardship, of what we are losing with such heedless scramble for 'efficiency'. Herewith:

1. End the phoney markets

Abolish the entire marketisation of NHS Healthcare and its apparatus of purchaser-provider splits, autarkic Trusts, financially-based commissioning, payment by results, financial penalties for comparative underperformance etc. The evidence of benefit is sparse. The evidence of inefficiency, waste, corruption, perversion and human inimicality is vast.

2. Disarm REMIC

REMIC (remote management, inspection and compliance) needs substantial disarmament. Having 'police presence' is very different to living in a police state. Forensic-type inspections should be reserved for practices/institutions where there is real evidence of hazard or failure. Generally pre-emptive quality-control works poorly throughout the welfare system, yet the economic and human costs are very high.

3. Stop the closure of small, popular general practices

These often provide the best Pastoral Healthcare from an ethos of vocational practice. Most outlying curative treatment requirements can be provided via a hub-and-spoke model. Encourage and foster such practices rather than regulating them out of existence.

4. Bring back General Physicians

General Physicians used to service the bulk of hospital medical requirements, calling in tertiary specialists only with very doubtful or refractory cases. Despite the endless advances in medical care this is still largely workable and advantageous: it clarifies and simplifies clinical responsibility, anchors personal continuity of care both for patients and their attendant GPs, and makes clinical work both more integrated and personally satisfying.

5. Abolish Geriatrics

Most people who go into hospital are old and likely to have multiple age-related conditions. So why have a separate specialty? Almost all, in the first instance, should be cared for by General Physicians aided – of course – in matters of rehabilitation, social care and tertiary specialist knowledge.

6. Bring back Consultant-led Firms

This almost always helps (small) group cohesion, affiliation, identity and belonging by restoring family-type dynamics: older practitioners feel they have 'children' to care for, younger practitioners feel they have 'parents' to guide, protect and care for them. Personal continuity of care becomes much more possible and gratifying.

7. Bring back smaller, more local, lower-tech hospitals

Most hospital admissions are for older people needing lower-tech care, more locally, when the at-home services have failed. They can be looked after by general-physician teams on familiar wards with far easier integration, personal continuity of care, work satisfaction and economy. Giant, distant high-tech hospitals would exist for major surgical and higher-tech medical problems.

8. Bring back Nursing Schools

The abolition of Nursing Schools deprived hospitals of senses of belonging, affiliation, loyalty, familiarity and community. The loss of *esprit de corps* has profound effects on recruitment, retention … and nursing care. Giant, generic universities can still be used for certain types of academic instruction – which could be pooled with other Nursing Schools – but the role of universities would be thus relegated and restricted. Smaller, provincial hospitals could be Nursing School-annexed to larger ones.

9. Break up Medical Schools into more but smaller units

This has similarities to point 8, above. The ever-larger size of medical schools has led to afflictions of Gigantism and nobody-knows-anybody syndromes. This is a bad way to start. Restoring smaller scales can mitigate or reverse many of these problems. As with nursing schools, some specialist knowledge and activities can be pooled and shared.

Epilogue - a riposte to Marx

Reforming the NHS from Within begins with the famous quote from Karl Marx in 1845:

"Philosophers have only interpreted the world in various ways; the point is to change it."

However, we may finish here instead, by considering the wisdom of caution. It is easy to understand Marx's impatience with inaction; a lot of us struggle with this. But what happens when our urge to change far exceeds our understanding?

For seventy years successive Officers of State in Soviet Russia quoted Marx often: they knew what-had-to-be-done, yet seemed not to know what they did not know about human nature. And so then they did not care. The human cost was massive.

But it seems this is a difficult lesson. It is a hundred and seventy-four years since Marx wrote this, and a hundred and one years since the Russian Revolution. Yet still we struggle with the same seductive folly of accelerating change, while leaving our human understanding further and further behind.

The Soviet system did not understand the individual's need for autonomy, initiative and privacy. The current NHS regime – that now captained by neoliberal industrialisation – seems not to understand communities' need for personal vocation, meaning and relationships.

The Soviet system became doomed by this blindness; hopefully our NHS can broaden its human vision before similar exhaustion and demise.

Photo: The Road West, US 54 in Southern New Mexico. Dorothea Lange, 1938

ABOUT THE AUTHOR

David Zigmond is a veteran NHS medical practitioner who has, increasingly, devoted himself to repersonalising the NHS. This has been fuelled by his perception of the last three decades of serial reforms and systematisations: each seems to squeeze yet more intelligence, life and humanity from our healthcare interactions – both with colleagues and patients.

Zigmond has worked as a frontline NHS doctor for the better (and worst) part of fifty years. His two main jobs have been as a traditional small practice family doctor and a large hospital psychiatrist and psychotherapist: in all of these he came to see (the now-imperilled) personal continuity of care as vital to much of our best care. Throughout this time he has spent the smaller fraction of his time working as a private psychotherapist.

For many years Zigmond has written about his wide-ranging experiences and his ideas of how to make sense of them. This has been contiguous to his teaching of healthcarers and psychotherapists.

Many of his writings can be found on his website at:

http://www.marco-learningsystems.com/pages/david-zigmond/david-zigmond.html

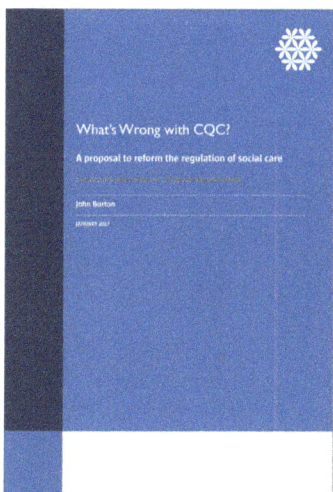

You may also be interested in:

What's Wrong with CQC?

In this paper John Burton explains why the Care Quality Commission (CQC) is unable to effectively safeguard standards for adult social care.

This paper is available to read at:
www.centreforwelfarereform.org

PUBLISHING INFORMATION

The Perils of Industrialised Healthcare © David Zigmond 2019
Adapted from a design by Henry Iles
All rights reserved.
First published August 2019
ISBN print: 978-1-912712-19-9
36 pp.

No part of this paper may be reproduced in any form without permission from the publisher, except for the quotation of brief passages in reviews.
The Perils of Industrialised Healthcare is published by the Centre for Welfare Reform.

CENTRE FOR WELFARE REFORM

The Centre for Welfare Reform is an independent research and development network. Its aim is to transform the current welfare state so that it supports citizenship, family and community. It works by developing and sharing social innovations and influencing government and society to achieve necessary reforms.

To find out more visit: www.centreforwelfarereform.org

Subscribe to our monthly email newsletter: bit.ly/subscribe-cfwr

Follow us on twitter: @CforWR

Find us on Facebook: @centreforwelfarereform

www.ingramcontent.com/pod-product-compliance
Lightning Source LLC
Chambersburg PA
CBHW061106210326
41597CB00022B/3995